Glad in HIS Presence

David's Revelation of GOD's Love & Mercy

Gerard Assey

Glad in HIS Presence:
David's Revelation of GOD's Love & Mercy

By

Gerard Assey

Published by:
Gerard Assey
19/18, Palli Arasan Street
Anna Nagar East
Chennai - 600 102

ISBN: 978-81-985691-6-5

Table of Contents

Preface

Have you ever wondered what made David so special? Why did God call him *"a man after My own heart"* (Acts 13:22), despite his failures and shortcomings? What set him apart from kings, prophets, and warriors who lived before and after him?

This book: **"Glad in HIS Presence: *David's Revelation of GOD's Love & Mercy*"** is an invitation to journey into the life of David—not just as a historical figure, but as a man who deeply understood the heart of God. It is not merely a collection of stories about a shepherd boy turned king; it is a revelation of God's presence, His mercy, and His power at work in an ordinary man who dared to trust Him completely.

David's life was full of contradictions—he was both a warrior and a worshipper, a king and a fugitive, a sinner and a saint. He experienced triumphs that shook kingdoms and failures that broke his own heart. And yet, in everything, he always ran back to God. That is what made him different. That is what makes his story worth studying today.

Why This Book?

This book is not meant to be a dry theological study or a mere retelling of Bible stories. It is meant to bring David's journey to life in a way that speaks to your own.

Each chapter explores a different aspect of David's relationship with God—his worship, his choices, his failures, his victories, and most importantly, his

pursuit of God's presence. Alongside David's story, we will see how the truths of his life are echoed in the New Testament and in the lives of people today.
We will not just learn about David—we will learn about ourselves.

- ✓ *What does it mean to seek God with all our hearts?*
- ✓ *How do we respond when we fall short?*
- ✓ *Can worship really change our lives?*
- ✓ *How do we live daily in God's presence?*

These are the questions that will guide us. And as we explore David's life, we will find the answers not just in his story, but in our own relationship with God.

An Invitation to Encounter God

This book is not just about gaining knowledge; it is about encountering the same living God that David knew. The same God who led David as a shepherd in the fields and as a king in the palace is still leading us today. His mercy is still available. His presence is still powerful. His love is still transforming lives.
As you read, I encourage you to go beyond just understanding David—let his life challenge you to draw closer to God. Let his mistakes remind you of grace. Let his victories stir up faith. Let his worship inspire a deeper hunger for God's presence in your own life.
May this book not just be another reading experience but a spiritual journey—one that brings you closer to the heart of the One who never stops pursuing us.
Welcome to the journey.

May you, like David, become a person after God's own heart.

Chapter 1:
The Joy of Being in God's Presence

David's words in Psalm 122:1 echo with such depth and emotion that they demand our attention: *"I was glad when they said to me, 'Let us go to the house of the Lord.'"*

These are not the words of a man burdened by obligation, nor of someone who is indifferent to worship. No, these are the words of a king—one who had tasted both the heights of victory and the depths of personal failure—yet still found his greatest joy in drawing near to God. But why was David so overjoyed at the idea of entering God's presence? What was it about worship that filled him with gladness?

To understand David's joy, we must step into his shoes for a moment.

David's Joy: More Than Just a Ritual

David was not born into priestly privilege, nor was he considered among the righteous elite of Israel. In fact, by strict Levitical law, he should never have been permitted in the assembly of the Lord. Deuteronomy 23:3 states: *"No Ammonite or Moabite or any of their descendants may enter the assembly of the Lord, not even in the tenth generation."*

David, the son of Jesse, carried within him Moabite blood through his great-great-grandmother Ruth. The Moabites were historically known as enemies of Israel, a people marked by their hostility toward God's chosen nation. And yet, David—a man who by law should have been kept outside—was not only welcomed but anointed as king.

Imagine the weight of that revelation.

David had no right to be in God's presence. But God broke the law for him because His mercy was greater than any restriction. David wasn't glad just because he had an opportunity to attend a religious gathering—he was ecstatic because he knew he didn't deserve to be there, yet he was invited anyway. His joy wasn't about the location of worship but the invitation itself.

It's the same kind of joy a man feels when he walks free from a prison sentence he should have rightfully served. Or the joy of a woman who has been estranged from her family for years but is suddenly welcomed home with open arms.

Why Does Worship Bring Joy?

David's joy wasn't based on a ritual, but on a relationship. Worship was not a routine for him—it was an encounter. And that encounter changed everything.

In today's world, we often see two types of worshipers:

- ✓ *Those who attend church out of habit.*
- ✓ *Those who enter with expectation.*

The first group sees worship as a duty; the second sees it as a privilege. David belonged to the latter. Every time he approached God, he did so with the anticipation of meeting Someone who loved him despite his failures.

Take, for instance, the story of Mary of Bethany in Luke 7:36-50. She was a woman with a sinful reputation. When she entered the house of a Pharisee to anoint Jesus' feet, she wasn't concerned about the judgmental stares or religious protocols. Why? Because she wasn't there to impress men—

she was there for Jesus. And when Jesus looked at her, He didn't see her past. He saw her heart.

She left that place forgiven and whole, her sorrow replaced by joy. Worship does that. It transforms. It lifts. It restores.

Real-life Example: Imagine a man named Samuel who had walked away from God for years. Guilt weighed on him, and he felt unworthy to even step into a church. But one day, something in him longed to go back. As he walked through the church doors, he expected condemnation, but instead, he was met with warmth. As the worship music began, Samuel felt tears streaming down his face—not out of sorrow, but relief. God's presence filled the room, and in that moment, Samuel knew that, like David, he was welcome in God's house, not because of what he had done, but because of who God was.

Jesus: Our Open Door to God's Presence

If David—under the Old Covenant—could rejoice in God's presence despite his Moabite heritage, how much more should we rejoice under the New Covenant?

In Hebrews 10:19-22, we read: *"Therefore, brothers and sisters, since we have confidence to enter the Most Holy Place by the blood of Jesus, by a new and living way opened for us through the curtain, that is, His body… let us draw near to God with a sincere heart and with the full assurance that faith brings."*

David had limited access to the presence of God—he could not enter the Holy of Holies, where God's glory dwelled. But Jesus changed everything.

When Christ died, the veil in the temple was torn in two (Matthew 27:51), symbolizing that we were no longer separated from God. Unlike David, we don't have to wait for a temple gathering to experience His presence. We don't need a priest to intercede on our behalf. We don't need to prove ourselves worthy. Through Jesus, we have direct and unlimited access to the Father.

Imagine a young child running into their father's office without hesitation. They don't need an appointment. They don't need credentials. They are welcomed simply because they are their father's child. That's what Jesus secured for us.

No longer do we have to wonder if we are worthy—Jesus has made us worthy.

No longer do we have to approach with fear—Jesus invites us to come with confidence.

No longer do we have to earn our place—Jesus has already paid for it.

The Joy That Cannot Be Taken Away

David's joy was not based on his circumstances, but on his revelation of who God was. He went through deep trials—he was hunted by Saul, betrayed by his own son, and suffered personal failures. But he always ran back to God.

In the same way, our joy in worship is not dictated by life's ups and downs. Worship isn't just for the good days—it's for the broken days, the uncertain days, the desperate days. Because joy isn't found in perfect circumstances; it's found in His presence.

Psalm 16:11 says: *"You will show me the path of life; in Your presence is fullness of joy; at Your right hand are pleasures forevermore."*

When we come before God—whether in a grand church or a quiet bedroom—we are stepping into a joy that is eternal, unshaken, and unbreakable.

David understood this. Do we?

Today, we are invited, just as David was, to experience the overwhelming, life-changing joy of God's presence. It is not for the religiously perfect, the morally elite, or the spiritually accomplished. It is for the broken, the unworthy, the Moabites, the sinners, the outcasts—for you and me.
And that… is why we are glad.

Reflection:

- ✓ *Have you ever felt unworthy to enter God's presence?*
- ✓ *What would change if you fully embraced the truth that Jesus has already made you worthy?*
- ✓ *How can you approach worship with the same joy and expectation that David had?*

Take a moment today to step into His presence—not as a religious act, but as a child running to their Father. You will find joy that no one can take away.

Chapter 2: David's Background – An Unlikely Choice

David's story is one of the most compelling accounts of God's grace, sovereignty, and redemption. He was not born into greatness, nor was he the most obvious choice for kingship. Yet, God chose him—not because of his pedigree or qualifications, but because of his heart.

When we think of David, we often picture the mighty warrior-king, the slayer of Goliath, the man after God's own heart. But before the throne, before the battlefield, before the songs of victory, David was just a shepherd boy—overlooked by men but handpicked by God. And even more astonishingly, David carried within him a lineage that should have disqualified him from even standing in God's presence.

David's Moabite Ancestry – A Disqualifying Lineage

To understand the depth of David's unlikeliness as a choice for king, we need to look at his family history. His great-grandmother was Ruth, a Moabite woman.

The Moabites were not an honored people in Israel. They were descendants of Lot and his eldest daughter (Genesis 19:30-38)—a lineage that originated in scandal and sin. Worse still, the Moabites were enemies of Israel, known for their idolatry and corruption. When the Israelites were journeying to the Promised Land, the Moabites refused them passage and even hired the prophet Balaam to curse them (Numbers 22-24).

Because of this hostility, God declared in Deuteronomy 23:3: *"No Ammonite or Moabite or any of their descendants may enter the assembly of the Lord, not even in the tenth generation."*
This was a divine law—Moabites were permanently excluded from worshiping among God's people. And yet, David, the future king of Israel, was only four generations removed from a Moabite woman.
How did this happen?
The answer is found in the story of Ruth.

Ruth: The Moabite Woman Who Found Favor with God

The book of Ruth tells the extraordinary story of a Moabite woman who, through sheer faith and devotion, became part of God's redemptive plan.
Ruth was married to an Israelite man, but when he died, she was left as a widow in a foreign land. She had every reason to return to her Moabite people, but instead, she chose to follow her mother-in-law, Naomi, back to Israel. In Ruth 1:16, she declared:
"Where you go I will go, and where you stay I will stay. Your people will be my people and your God my God."
This decision was radical. She was forsaking her own heritage and embracing the God of Israel—even when it meant living as a foreigner among those who looked down on her.
Through divine providence, Ruth found favor in the eyes of Boaz, a righteous man of Israel. He married her, and their son Obed became the grandfather of David (Ruth 4:13-17).
By Jewish law, David's Moabite blood should have kept him from ever entering the temple, let alone

becoming king. And yet, God broke His own rule to anoint him.

God Breaking His Own Rule – A Testament of Grace

This is one of the greatest pictures of God's grace in the Old Testament.

David should have been excluded. But God, in His sovereignty, made an exception. Why? Because grace always triumphs over the law.

This moment foreshadowed the work of Jesus Christ, who would later shatter all barriers of exclusion. Where the law once dictated who could and could not approach God, Jesus came to open the way for everyone. Just as David was an unworthy choice made worthy by God's grace, so too are we—once sinners, now called sons and daughters of the King.

This principle is woven throughout Scripture. God consistently chooses the unlikely.

God's Pattern: Choosing the Unlikely

David was not the first, nor the last, of God's unexpected choices.

Moses was a man who stammered and was full of self-doubt. When God called him to lead Israel out of Egypt, Moses protested, saying, *"I am slow of speech and tongue" (Exodus 4:10).* But God chose him anyway.

Gideon was a man consumed by fear. When the angel of the Lord appeared to him, Gideon was hiding, terrified of the Midianites. Yet, God called him a "mighty warrior" and used him to deliver Israel (Judges 6:12).

Rahab was a prostitute in Jericho, a woman whose past should have disqualified her from any role in

God's plan. But when she chose to hide the Israelite spies and put her faith in God, she was redeemed, becoming part of the lineage of Jesus Himself (Joshua 2, Matthew 1:5).

God has never been interested in picking the obvious choices. He delights in raising up the unexpected, the unworthy, the overlooked. Why? Because when He chooses the weak, the broken, and the outcasts, His glory is revealed all the more.

David was a shepherd, not a warrior. A boy, not a king. A descendant of Moab, not of priestly lineage. And yet, he was handpicked by God to lead Israel.

Real-Life Example: God Still Chooses the Unlikely

In our world today, we still see God working through the most unexpected people.

Consider the story of Daniel, a young man raised in poverty. Society had written him off—he grew up in a broken home, surrounded by crime and addiction. He barely made it through school and had no real future ahead of him.

But one day, he encountered God in a way that changed everything. He started attending a small church where someone saw his potential and mentored him. Over time, he grew into a leader—passionate, wise, and deeply rooted in faith. Years later, the very community that had once counted him out looked to him for guidance. He became a pastor, ministering to the broken and forgotten.

Just like David, just like Moses, just like Rahab—Daniel was an unlikely choice. But God's grace rewrote his story.

God's Message to Us: You Are Not Disqualified

David's background teaches us one thing loud and clear: God does not choose people based on their past—He chooses them based on His purpose.

If you've ever felt disqualified because of your history, your mistakes, or what others have said about you, remember this:

- ✓ *David was chosen despite being a Moabite descendant.*
- ✓ *Moses was chosen despite his insecurities.*
- ✓ *Gideon was chosen despite his fear.*
- ✓ *Rahab was chosen despite her past.*
- ✓ *And you are chosen, too.*
- ✓ *God does not call the qualified—He qualifies the called.*

The next time you doubt whether God can use you, remember David. Remember Ruth. Remember the long line of unlikely choices that God has used to change history. His grace is greater than your past, and His calling on your life is unshakable.

Reflection:

- ✓ *Have you ever felt unworthy or disqualified from being used by God?*
- ✓ *How does David's story encourage you to see yourself through God's eyes rather than the world's?*
- ✓ *What would change in your life if you fully believed that God chooses you, not because of your qualifications, but because of His grace?*

Today, God is still in the business of picking the unexpected and turning them into world changers. If you're feeling like an unlikely choice—take heart. You're in good company.

Chapter 3:
Ruth's Choice & The Heart of God

Some choices seem small when we make them. They don't always come with grand announcements or flashing lights. But those choices, when aligned with God's heart, can change everything. The story of Ruth is one of devotion, redemption, and divine orchestration. It is a testament to the power of a single decision—one that not only altered her life but shaped the course of history, leading to the birth of Jesus Christ Himself.

At the heart of it all was one choice: Ruth's decision to leave behind everything familiar and follow Naomi into the unknown.

Ruth's Decision to Follow Naomi – A Heart Aligned with God

The book of Ruth opens with tragedy. Naomi, an Israelite woman, had traveled to Moab with her husband and two sons to escape a famine in Israel. While in Moab, her husband died. Later, both of her sons—who had married Moabite women, Orpah and Ruth—also died.

Naomi, now widowed and childless, decided to return to Israel. She urged her daughters-in-law to stay in Moab, where they would have better chances of remarrying and starting fresh. Orpah, after much weeping, made the logical choice—she returned to her people.

But Ruth refused to leave.

Her response in Ruth 1:16-17 is one of the most powerful declarations of faith in the Bible:

"Do not urge me to leave you or to return from following you. For where you go, I will go, and where you lodge, I will lodge. Your people shall be my people, and your God my God. Where you die, I will die, and there will I be buried. May the Lord do so to me and more also if anything but death parts me from you."

This was not just loyalty to Naomi—it was a declaration of faith in the God of Israel.

Ruth was a Moabite, an outsider, someone who had no place among God's chosen people. Yet, she was willing to forsake her heritage, her gods, and her comfort to follow Naomi into uncertainty.

It was a decision of the heart. It wasn't based on what was logical or beneficial for her. It was driven by an unexplainable draw toward the true God.

This is how God chooses people—not based on where they come from, but on where their hearts are directed.

One Choice Changed an Entire Lineage – From an Outsider to the Bloodline of Jesus

Ruth's choice did not just affect her life—it rewrote history.

When she and Naomi arrived in Bethlehem, they were two widowed women with no resources. In those times, a woman without a husband had little hope for provision. But Ruth, determined to care for Naomi, went to work gleaning grain in the fields—picking up what the harvesters left behind.

This is where she met Boaz, a wealthy and godly man.

Boaz took notice of Ruth, not just because of her beauty but because of her character. He had heard of her loyalty to Naomi and her decision to follow the

God of Israel. Because of this, he extended kindness and protection to her.

In time, through a divine arrangement, Boaz married Ruth. Their union led to the birth of Obed, who became the grandfather of King David (Ruth 4:13-17). And from David's lineage came Jesus Christ.

Imagine that.

A Moabite widow, someone who should have been excluded from God's people, became a key link in the Messianic lineage.

This is the heart of God—to take the unlikely and make them essential to His plan.

It all started with one act of faith.

Ruth had no idea that her decision to follow Naomi would lead to such generational impact. She had no prophecy, no angelic visitation, no divine sign. She simply made a choice, based on faith, to follow God. And because of that, she became part of the greatest redemption story ever told.

The Power of God's Redemption in Changing Destinies

Ruth's story is not just about her redemption—it is about God's pattern of redeeming the unworthy, the outcast, and the broken.

Throughout the Bible, we see this again and again:

- ✓ Joseph was betrayed by his own brothers, sold into slavery, and imprisoned unfairly. But because he remained faithful, God raised him up to become a ruler in Egypt, saving countless lives (Genesis 50:20).
- ✓ Rahab was a prostitute in Jericho. Yet, because she chose to help the Israelite spies, God saved her and placed her in the lineage of Jesus (Joshua 2, Matthew 1:5).

- ✓ Peter denied Jesus three times at His most critical moment. But God's grace restored him, making him a pillar of the early church (John 21:15-17).

God is not limited by our pasts. He is not restricted by who society says we are. When He redeems, He does not just fix things—He rebuilds them better than before.

Ruth, the Moabite widow, became an honored matriarch in God's plan.

Joseph, the rejected brother, became a ruler of Egypt.

Rahab, the outcast prostitute, became part of the Messianic line.

And today, God is still writing redemption stories.

Modern-Day Testimonies of Lives Transformed by One Act of Faith

This same power of redemption is at work today.

Consider the story of Rachel, a young woman raised in a home of abuse and addiction. By the time she was a teenager, she had run away from home, dropped out of school, and was living on the streets. She had no hope, no future.

One night, she wandered into a small church. She didn't plan to stay—she only wanted to warm up from the cold. But as she sat in the back, something stirred inside her. She heard the pastor talking about Jesus' love for the broken, how God takes the rejected and makes them His own.

That night, she made a choice—she gave her life to Christ.

It didn't change everything overnight. But slowly, God restored her. She was taken in by a Christian family, went back to school, and eventually became a social worker. Today, she runs a ministry for young women who are trapped in the same cycles she once was. Like Ruth, one choice changed everything.

God's Invitation to Us

Ruth's story is not just an ancient tale—it is an invitation.

God is still calling people to make bold choices of faith. To step out of the familiar, out of their past, out of their limitations, and into His plan.

You don't have to be perfect. You don't have to have the right background. You don't have to be the strongest, the smartest, or the most qualified. You just have to say yes.

One act of faith can:

- ✓ *Rewrite your destiny.*
- ✓ *Change your family's future.*
- ✓ *Make you part of something far greater than yourself.*

Ruth's journey began with a choice. Today, what choice is God calling you to make?

Reflection:

- ✓ *What decision is God asking you to make today that requires faith?*
- ✓ *Have you ever felt like an outsider, unworthy of God's blessings?*
- ✓ *How does Ruth's story encourage you to trust God, even when the road ahead is uncertain?*

Remember: Faithful choices lead to divine destinies.

God is still in the business of taking the least expected and making them a part of His greatest story.

Are you ready to take that step?

Chapter 4: The Revelation of God's Love and Mercy

There are few figures in the Bible as complex as David. He was a warrior, a poet, a shepherd, a king, a worshiper, and yet, at times, a sinner of the worst kind. He knew the depths of failure, but more importantly, he knew the height of God's mercy.

David's life was a paradox—he committed great sins, yet he was called a man after God's own heart (1 Samuel 13:14). How could that be? How could someone who had broken so many of God's commands still be deeply loved and favored by Him?

The answer lies in David's revelation of God's mercy. He understood something that many never fully grasp: God's mercy is greater than human failure.

Why Did David Always Run to God?

Most people, when they sin, run from God. They hide in shame, much like Adam and Eve did in the Garden of Eden (Genesis 3:8). They believe their mistakes make them unworthy to approach Him.

But David was different.

When he sinned, he didn't run away—he ran toward God. He didn't make excuses. He didn't try to justify his actions. Instead, he fell on his face in brokenness and cried out for mercy.

One of the most powerful examples of this is found in Psalm 51, a song of repentance written after David had committed one of the greatest moral failures in history—his affair with Bathsheba and the murder of her husband, Uriah.

David had everything—wealth, power, a thriving kingdom—yet he still fell into lust, adultery, deception, and murder.
When the prophet Nathan confronted him (2 Samuel 12), David didn't deny it. He didn't blame others. He simply said, "I have sinned against the Lord" (2 Samuel 12:13).
And then he wrote these words: *"Have mercy on me, O God, according to Your unfailing love; according to Your great compassion, blot out my transgressions. Wash away all my iniquity and cleanse me from my sin."* — Psalm 51:1-2
David understood something about God that many still struggle to believe: God's love and mercy are greater than our worst mistakes.
This is why David always ran to God—he knew that only God could cleanse him.

His Sins Were Great, But His Understanding of God's Mercy Was Greater

David had seen God's mercy firsthand. His life was full of second chances, undeserved favor, and restoration.
He knew that God's love was not based on his perfection, but on God's nature.
David understood the mercy of God because he himself had been on the receiving end of grace that defied logic. Consider his own heritage.

God's Mercy Overrules His Own Laws – The Moabite King

By law, David should not have been king.
Deuteronomy 23:3 explicitly states: *"No Ammonite or Moabite or any of their descendants may enter the*

assembly of the Lord, even down to the tenth generation."

Yet David, a descendant of Ruth the Moabite, became the chosen king of Israel.

God broke His own law to establish David. Why? Because mercy triumphs over judgment (James 2:13).

David's own life was a testimony to the grace of God—a reminder that God's plan is not limited by human rules.

How often do we think we are disqualified from God's calling because of our past? How many times do we believe our failures have canceled our destiny?

But David's story proves that God's mercy overrides even the most impossible barriers.

New Testament Parallel: The Prodigal Son (Luke 15:11-32)

Jesus illustrated the same truth in the parable of the Prodigal Son.

A young man, full of pride and rebellion, demanded his inheritance early. He wasted it on wild living, eventually finding himself broke and starving in a pigpen—the lowest place a Jewish man could be.

Realizing he had no other option, he decided to return to his father. But he did not expect to be restored—he only hoped to be taken back as a servant.

However, before he even reached home, his father saw him from a distance and ran to him.

The father didn't wait for an apology. He didn't demand repayment. He simply embraced him and restored him fully (Luke 15:20-24).

That is God's mercy.

David knew this mercy firsthand. And Jesus came to prove that the heart of the Father has never changed.

Real-Life Story: Someone Who Encountered Deep Grace and Transformation

Meet Samuel.

He was raised in church but walked away as a teenager. He got involved with the wrong crowd, spiraled into addiction, and made choices that destroyed his family.

By the time he was in his mid-30s, Samuel had lost everything—his marriage, his career, and his dignity. He was living on the streets, convinced that God had given up on him.

One night, he stumbled into an old church. He sat in the back, ashamed to even look at the altar. As the pastor spoke about God's mercy, Samuel felt something stir inside him.

For the first time in years, he prayed: "*God, if You can still love me, if You can still use me… I'm Yours.*"

That was the beginning of his restoration.

Over time, Samuel found healing, got clean, and reconciled with his family. Today, he runs an outreach ministry for homeless addicts, helping them experience the same mercy that changed his life.

Like David, like the prodigal son—he ran back to the Father, and the Father ran to meet him.

God's Invitation to You

David's story, the prodigal son's story, and Samuel's story all tell us the same truth:

You are never too far gone for God's mercy.

No sin is too great. No past is too dark. No mistake is beyond God's ability to redeem.

If you feel like you've failed, if you feel like you've disqualified yourself from God's love, remember David.

- ✓ Remember how he always ran back to God—and God always received him.
- ✓ Remember that Jesus told the story of the Father who runs to the broken.
- ✓ And remember that your story is not over.

The same God who restored David, who welcomed the prodigal, and who redeemed Samuel is waiting for you with open arms.

Run to Him. His mercy is greater than your failure.

Reflection:

- ✓ *Have you ever felt too far gone for God's mercy?*
- ✓ *What is holding you back from running back to Him?*
- ✓ *Do you believe that His mercy is greater than your worst failure?*

Let today be the day you stop running away and start running to God.

He is waiting.

Chapter 5:
Worship – The Heartbeat of David

If there is one word that defines David's relationship with God, it is worship. Before he was a warrior, before he was a king, before he was even known by men, he was a worshiper.

Worship was David's foundation. It was his language, his weapon, his source of strength, and his greatest expression of love for God. To David, worship wasn't just singing songs—it was his very lifeline to God.

And this is what set him apart.

Most kings in history were known for their military might, wealth, or political strategies, but David was different. He was a man after God's own heart (1 Samuel 13:14), and his heart beat to the rhythm of worship.

David's Life as a Worshiper Before He Was a Warrior

Long before David became famous for slaying Goliath, he was a shepherd boy, alone in the fields, tending his father's sheep. But he was never truly alone—because he had learned to fill the silence with worship.

Imagine David as a young boy, sitting under the open sky, his harp in his hands, singing to the God he loved. No audience, no recognition, no stage—just a boy and his Creator.

This is where David's faith was forged.

While his older brothers trained in battle, David trained in worship.

While they learned to wield swords and shields, David learned to wield songs and psalms.

And this is the reason God chose him.
When the prophet Samuel came to anoint the next king of Israel, Jesse, David's father, didn't even bother calling him. David was forgotten by men, but never forgotten by God.
And why? Because God doesn't choose as men do.
"Man looks at the outward appearance, but the Lord looks at the heart." —1 Samuel 16:7
And David's heart was full of worship.
This is why, when the time came to face Goliath, David didn't cower in fear. He had spent years in the presence of God, and he knew that no giant could ever be bigger than his God.
His faith was not in himself, but in the God he had worshiped in secret.

The Power of Worship to Transform Situations
One of the most iconic moments of worship in David's life was the day he brought the Ark of the Covenant back to Jerusalem.
The Ark represented God's presence, and David was so overwhelmed with joy that he couldn't contain himself.
"David danced before the Lord with all his might." —2 Samuel 6:14
It wasn't a quiet, formal ceremony. It wasn't stiff or reserved. It was uncontrollable, passionate, extravagant worship.
And not everyone understood it.
His wife, Michal, watched from a window and despised him for acting so undignified (2 Samuel 6:16).
But David didn't care about human opinions.

He wasn't worshiping for people—he was worshiping for God.
And this is what true worship does—it shifts the focus off ourselves and onto the One who deserves all honor.
It transforms situations, atmospheres, and even our own hearts.

Worship and Intimacy with God – Beyond Music, It's a Lifestyle

For David, worship was not just music—it was a way of life.
His psalms reflect the rawness of his emotions. He worshiped when he was happy and when he was broken.

- ✓ When he was victorious, he sang praises.
- ✓ When he was afraid, he sang for protection.
- ✓ When he was repentant, he sang for mercy.

Worship wasn't a performance for David—it was his communication with God.
This is why worship is so powerful—it takes the focus off our problems and shifts it to God's power.

New Testament Parallel: Paul & Silas in Prison

The power of worship is not limited to David's time.
In the New Testament, we see Paul and Silas locked up in a dark, cold prison. They had been beaten and chained for preaching the Gospel.
Most people would have complained. Most would have questioned God.
But not Paul and Silas.
"About midnight Paul and Silas were praying and singing hymns to God, and the other prisoners were listening to them." —Acts 16:25
In the worst of circumstances, they chose to worship.

And what happened?
"Suddenly there was such a violent earthquake that the foundations of the prison were shaken. At once all the prison doors flew open, and everyone's chains came loose."
—Acts 16:26
Worship doesn't just change us—it changes everything around us.
When we worship, chains break, doors open, and the impossible becomes possible.
This is why David danced with all his might—because he knew the power of worship.
And this is why, even today, worship remains one of the most powerful weapons we have.

Practical Section: How to Cultivate a Heart of Worship Daily
Worship is not just for Sundays. It's a lifestyle.
So how do we develop a heart of worship like David?

- ✓ Start Your Day with Worship
  Before checking your phone or worrying about the day ahead, take a moment to acknowledge God. Play a worship song, sing a simple prayer, or just say, "Lord, I praise You today."
- ✓ Make Worship Personal
  Worship is not about performance—it's about connection. Whether you're in a church or alone in your room, worship like it's just you and God.
- ✓ Worship in All Circumstances
  Like David, Paul, and Silas, worship even when life is hard. Worship when you don't feel like it. Worship is a declaration that God is greater than your struggles.

- ✓ Let Worship Be More Than Music
  True worship is obedience. It's living a life that honors God—not just in song, but in how we speak, how we love, how we serve, and how we live.
- ✓ Keep a Heart of Gratitude
  Worship flows from a thankful heart. The more we focus on God's goodness, the more worship becomes natural.

God's Invitation to You

David was called a man after God's own heart—not because he was perfect, but because he was a worshiper.

God is still looking for worshipers today—people who will love Him, seek Him, and glorify Him in every season of life.

Do you want to be like David?

Then start worshiping like David.

Not just with songs, but with your heart, your life, and your actions.

And as you do, you will see the power of worship transform your life—just as it did for David, Paul, and countless others who have encountered the presence of God.

So lift your hands, lift your voice, and worship with all your might.

God is waiting.

Chapter 6:
Running to God, Not From Him

There are two ways people respond to failure. Some run away from God, hiding in shame, guilt, and regret, convinced that they are beyond redemption. Others run toward Him, broken but willing to be restored.

David, despite his many flaws and failures, was a man who always ran to God. He did not let his mistakes push him away from his Creator. Instead, he turned toward Him, knowing that God's mercy was greater than his sin.

This is what made David different from so many others.

Many men in the Bible failed, but not all of them found restoration. Saul, the first king of Israel, was rejected because he tried to cover up his sin rather than repent (1 Samuel 15:10-26). Judas, one of Jesus' disciples, fell into despair and took his own life instead of seeking forgiveness (Matthew 27:3-5).

But David?

David knew where to run. He knew that even when he had fallen, God was still his refuge.

David's Response to Failure – Running Toward God, Not Away

One of the darkest moments in David's life was his sin with Bathsheba.

David had everything. He was king, victorious in battle, loved by his people, and deeply favored by God. But at the height of his success, he made a terrible choice.

It began with a look.

One evening, as he walked on his palace rooftop, he saw a woman bathing—Bathsheba, the wife of Uriah, one of his most loyal soldiers. Desire took over, and David sent for her.

That one moment of weakness turned into a chain reaction of sin.

Bathsheba became pregnant. To cover it up, David tried deception, calling Uriah home from battle so he would sleep with his wife. But Uriah, being honorable, refused to enjoy comfort while his fellow soldiers were still at war.

When David's first plan failed, he turned to something far worse.

He arranged for Uriah's death, placing him at the front lines where he would surely be killed. Once Uriah was dead, David took Bathsheba as his wife, thinking that no one would know.

But God saw everything.

And He sent Nathan the prophet to confront David.

Nathan told a parable about a rich man who stole a poor man's only lamb. When David reacted in anger, saying the man deserved death, Nathan looked at him and said:

"You are the man!" (2 Samuel 12:7)

At that moment, David could have run—he could have justified his actions, covered up his guilt, or let shame consume him.

But instead, he ran to God.

David's response was immediate and heartfelt:

"I have sinned against the Lord." (2 Samuel 12:13)

He didn't blame others. He didn't make excuses. He fell before God in brokenness, pleading for mercy.

This is why David was different.

He understood that failure was not the end when placed in God's hands.

God's Response to a Repentant Heart

Many people think that failure disqualifies them from God's love, but David's life shows us the opposite.

Though David sinned greatly, he also repented greatly.

He wrote Psalm 51, one of the most heartfelt prayers of repentance in the Bible.

"Have mercy on me, O God, according to Your unfailing love;
according to Your great compassion, blot out my transgressions." (Psalm 51:1)

David wasn't asking God to excuse his sin. He was asking for a clean heart, a renewed spirit, and a restored relationship with God.

And God, in His mercy, forgave him.

Yes, David still faced consequences—his child with Bathsheba died, and there was turmoil in his family—but God did not abandon him.

In fact, God still called David "a man after My own heart" (Acts 13:22).

How is that possible?

Because God looks at the heart.

David's heart, though it had stumbled, was always drawn back to God.

This is the beauty of grace—God does not define us by our worst moments, but by our willingness to return to Him.

New Testament Parallel: The Prodigal Son

David's story finds a powerful reflection in Jesus' parable of the Prodigal Son (Luke 15:11-32).

A young man, given everything by his father, took his inheritance and wasted it on reckless living. When he

finally hit rock bottom—hungry, alone, and feeding pigs—he realized his mistake.
He could have stayed away, convinced that he was too far gone. But instead, he chose to return home.
And what did his father do?
Did he punish him? Shame him? Reject him?
No.
"While he was still a long way off, his father saw him and was filled with compassion;
he ran to his son, threw his arms around him, and kissed him." (Luke 15:20)
God runs toward the repentant.
This is why David was never abandoned—because he never stopped running toward God.
And this is why, no matter what we have done, we can always return to the Father.

Real-Life Story: A Modern David
James had once been a passionate believer. He was active in church, led worship, and shared the Gospel wherever he went. But life took a turn, and slowly, he drifted.
First, it was small compromises—missing prayer, skipping church. Then, it became bigger decisions—unwise relationships, unhealthy habits. Before long, James was so far from God that he felt unworthy to return.
One night, after a particularly dark moment, he broke down. He sat alone in his room, overwhelmed by guilt, convinced that he had gone too far for God to forgive him.
But then, something stirred in his heart.
A verse he had memorized years ago came back to him:

"If we confess our sins, He is faithful and just to forgive us and cleanse us from all unrighteousness." (1 John 1:9)

For the first time in years, James fell to his knees and prayed. He poured out his heart, admitting his failures, pleading for mercy.

And at that moment, God met him.

It wasn't a thunderous voice or a dramatic vision—it was peace. A deep, unshakable peace, washing over him, reminding him that he was never beyond redemption.

That night, James began his journey back to God.

Like David, he had failed—but he ran toward God, and God restored him.

God's Invitation to You

No one is beyond God's mercy.

If David, an adulterer and murderer, could be forgiven and restored, then so can you.

If the Prodigal Son could come home and be embraced, then so can you.

If James, who walked away from his faith, could be welcomed back, then so can you.

God does not reject the broken—He heals them.

So if you've made mistakes, if you feel distant from God, if you're carrying shame and guilt, you have a choice.

- ✓ Will you run away and let your failures define you?
- ✓ Or will you run toward God and let His mercy restore you?

David ran to God—and found grace.

The Prodigal Son ran to his father—and found love.

And today, God is waiting for you to do the same.

Run to Him. He is waiting with open arms.

Chapter 7: The Presence of God – A Source of Power

David's life was marked by one defining pursuit—the presence of God. Unlike many kings who sought power, riches, or victory, David longed for God Himself. He understood that true strength did not come from military might or political strategy but from being near to the presence of the Almighty.

This was the secret to his success, the force that lifted him from a lowly shepherd boy to the greatest king in Israel's history.

But what does it mean to seek God's presence? And why did David prioritize it above all else?

To answer that, we must go back to where it all began.

Why Did David Seek God's Presence So Passionately?

David's journey to understanding the power of God's presence started in the fields.

As a young shepherd, he spent long, lonely nights tending his father's sheep. But David was not alone—he worshipped, he prayed, and he encountered God in the wilderness.

When a lion or bear attacked the flock, David fought them off, but he never took credit for his victories. He knew that the strength he displayed was not his own but came from the presence of God with him.

This became even clearer when he stood before Goliath.

While the entire Israelite army trembled in fear, David was unshaken. Not because of his skill with a sling, but because he had already experienced God's power in the past.

"You come against me with sword and spear and javelin, but I come against you in the name of the LORD Almighty!" (1 Samuel 17:45)

David's confidence came not from his ability, but from the presence of God.

This is what set him apart.

Many people believe in God, but few desire Him deeply. David longed for communion with God. He was not content with religious rituals—he wanted intimacy. This is why, even after becoming king, he never stopped seeking God's presence.

How God's Presence Empowered Him – From a Shepherd to a King

David's entire life was shaped by the presence of God.

When Samuel came to anoint a new king, he bypassed David's older, stronger brothers because God was not looking for outward strength, but inward devotion.

"The Lord does not look at the things people look at. People look at the outward appearance, but the Lord looks at the heart." (1 Samuel 16:7)

David's heart was set on God, and that is why he was chosen.

Throughout his life, this pattern continued.

He sought God before every battle (2 Samuel 5:19).

He refused to harm Saul, the Lord's anointed (1 Samuel 24:6), even when he had the chance.

He rejoiced in worship when bringing the Ark back to Jerusalem, caring more about God's presence than about his dignity as king (2 Samuel 6:14).
David's victories, wisdom, and favor came not from his talent, but from his closeness to God.

The Ark of the Covenant & David's Respect for It
David understood that God's presence was the true source of Israel's strength.
During his reign, one of his greatest desires was to bring the Ark of the Covenant back to Jerusalem.
The Ark represented the dwelling place of God among His people. It had been lost in battle and remained in a foreign land for years. But David could not rest knowing that God's presence was not in the center of Israel.
He gathered his men and set out to bring the Ark home, but something tragic happened.
During the journey, one of the men, Uzzah, touched the Ark when the oxen stumbled—and he was struck dead (2 Samuel 6:6-7).
David was terrified and confused. He had the right intention, but he had forgotten that God's presence must be approached with reverence.
For three months, the Ark remained in the house of Obed-Edom, and his household was blessed abundantly (2 Samuel 6:11). This confirmed to David that God's presence was not something to be feared—but something to be honored.
When David finally brought the Ark back to Jerusalem, he did it the right way, with worship, sacrifices, and joy.
As the Ark entered the city, David danced before the Lord with all his might (2 Samuel 6:14).

His wife, Michal, looked at him with disdain, embarrassed that the king would behave in such an undignified way. But David's response was powerful: *"I will celebrate before the Lord. I will become even more undignified than this!"* (2 Samuel 6:21-22)
David understood that no position, no title, and no amount of human honor compared to the presence of God.

New Testament Parallel: The Holy Spirit in Us Today
In the Old Testament, God's presence was contained in the Ark, but in the New Testament, everything changed.
When Jesus came, He promised something even greater:
"And I will ask the Father, and He will give you another Helper, to be with you forever—the Spirit of truth." (John 14:16-17)
The presence of God now lives within us through the Holy Spirit.
This is something David could only long for. In Psalm 51:11, after his sin, he prayed:
"Do not cast me from Your presence or take Your Holy Spirit from me."
David knew that God's presence was everything.
And today, we have something even more powerful than David did—the Spirit of God living within us.
The question is, do we value His presence the way David did?

Living Daily in God's Presence
David did not just seek God occasionally. He lived in God's presence every day.
How can we do the same?

Prioritize Worship – Worship is not just singing songs. It is a heart posture of surrender and love for God. David worshipped in the fields, in battle, and even in his palace. Make worship a daily practice.

Seek Him in Prayer – David consulted God before making decisions. Prayer should be our first response, not our last resort.

Treasure His Word – David meditated on God's law (Psalm 119:97). The more we fill ourselves with God's Word, the more His presence transforms us.

Walk in Obedience – God's presence is not just an experience; it is a way of life. Living in obedience keeps us close to Him.

Invite the Holy Spirit Daily – Unlike David, we do not have to go to a temple to find God. He is within us. A simple prayer—*"Holy Spirit, fill me today"*—can change everything.

A Real-Life Story: A Modern-Day David

Lucas was an ambitious businessman. He had built a successful career but found himself feeling empty. No matter how much money he made, something was missing.

One evening, he attended a church service. The worship team sang a song about hungering for God's presence. Something stirred in his heart.

For the first time in years, he realized—he had built his life on everything except God.

That night, he made a decision.

He began seeking God's presence daily. He started his mornings in prayer. He filled his car rides with worship. He asked the Holy Spirit to guide him in his work.

And everything changed.

His business flourished, but more importantly, his heart was full.
Like David, Lucas discovered that the greatest treasure was not success, but intimacy with God.

Conclusion: A Life in His Presence

David's life teaches us one thing—nothing is greater than the presence of God.
It is what gives us strength, wisdom, and joy. It transforms ordinary people into mighty leaders.
The question is, are we seeking Him like David did? Because when we do, everything changes.

Chapter 8:
From Outcast to Crowned King

The story of David is one of divine selection, of a boy ignored by his family yet chosen by God to lead a nation. It is a story that defies human expectations—a reminder that God's ways are higher than ours.

If there was ever a man who understood what it meant to be undervalued, overlooked, and cast aside, it was David. But his journey reveals a powerful truth: God does not choose as men choose. The world values strength, status, and influence, but God looks for something deeper—the heart.

Overlooked and Forgotten – David's Humble Beginnings

The scene was set in Bethlehem, a small, insignificant town that held no political power or military strength. It was here that God sent His prophet, Samuel, with a mission—to anoint a new king for Israel.

At that time, King Saul still sat on the throne, but his disobedience had cost him God's favor. The Lord had rejected Saul and was now raising up someone else—someone no one would expect.

Samuel arrived at the house of Jesse, a respected man in Bethlehem who had several strong, capable sons. Surely, one of them must be the future king!

When Jesse's eldest son, Eliab, stepped forward, he looked the part. He was tall, strong, and carried himself like a leader. Samuel, thinking as most men do, assumed he had found the one.

"Surely the Lord's anointed stands here before the Lord," Samuel thought (1 Samuel 16:6).

But God interrupted him with a powerful statement: *"Do not consider his appearance or his height, for I have rejected him. The Lord does not look at the things people look at. People look at the outward appearance, but the Lord looks at the heart."* (1 Samuel 16:7)

One by one, Jesse's sons passed before Samuel—seven in total. Yet God rejected them all.

Samuel was confused. He asked Jesse, "Are these all your sons?"

Only then did Jesse mention his youngest son, David.

David wasn't even invited to the gathering. In his father's eyes, he wasn't important enough to be considered for kingship. He was out in the fields, tending the sheep.

It was as if Jesse was saying, *"David? No, you must mean one of my older sons. David is just a boy."*

But Samuel insisted, "Send for him; we will not sit down until he arrives."

When David finally came in, God spoke immediately: *"Rise and anoint him; this is the one."* (1 Samuel 16:12)

Before his father, his brothers, and the prophet of God, David was anointed as the future king of Israel.

No one saw it coming. No one expected the boy tending sheep to be God's chosen ruler.

But God had seen what no one else did—a heart fully devoted to Him.

Man Sees the Outward, But God Sees the Heart

David's story is a powerful reminder that God's standards are not like ours.

The world honors wealth, beauty, status, and power. People are judged by their achievements and influence. But God is searching for something deeper.

David had no royal bloodline, no battlefield experience, and no leadership credentials. But what he did have was a heart that longed for God.

This is what set him apart.

Many people chase success, but few chase after God. Many seek recognition, but few seek to please the Lord.

David, long before he ever wore a crown, was a king in God's eyes because he had a heart fully surrendered to Him.

And this is still true today.

God is not looking for the most qualified, but for the most surrendered.

New Testament Parallel: Jesus Choosing the Outcasts

David's story is a perfect foreshadowing of how Jesus calls the unlikely.

When Jesus began His ministry, He did not seek out the religious elite, the scholars, or the powerful rulers.

Instead, He chose fishermen, tax collectors, and outcasts.

Peter, a simple fisherman, became the rock on which Christ built His church.

Matthew, a tax collector despised by his people, became one of the Gospel writers.

Mary Magdalene, a woman once bound by demons, was chosen to be the first to witness the risen Christ.

Jesus never picked people based on human standards. He saw what others could not—the potential of a surrendered heart.

The same was true for David. The world saw a shepherd, but God saw a king.

Real-Life Story: A Modern-Day David

Nathan had always been the one everyone overlooked.

Born into a struggling family in a small village, he never excelled in school. His teachers dismissed him, his classmates ignored him, and even his own parents never expected much from him.

At seventeen, he dropped out of school and started working at a local mechanic shop. No one saw potential in him.

But Nathan had one thing—a hunger for God.

He spent his lunch breaks reading the Bible. He prayed before every task, asking God for wisdom. He served faithfully in his small church, always eager to help.

Years passed, and something extraordinary happened.

A businessman, whose car Nathan had repaired, noticed his dedication and invited him to a leadership seminar. One opportunity led to another, and soon, Nathan was leading a team of young apprentices.

Before he knew it, he had started his own business—not just a successful company, but a place where young, overlooked men like himself could be trained and mentored.

The same people who had dismissed him now respected him.

Nathan's story is a modern reminder of David's journey. He was unnoticed by men but handpicked by God.

Today, he teaches young people that God does not need your credentials—He needs your heart.

The Call to the Overlooked

Maybe you have felt like David.

Maybe you've been dismissed, rejected, or underestimated. Maybe people have told you that you're not smart enough, strong enough, or experienced enough.

But God does not see you the way the world sees you.

- ✓ *Where others see a nobody, God sees a leader.*
- ✓ *Where others see a failure, God sees a future.*
- ✓ *Where others see a shepherd, God sees a king.*

David's story is proof that God raises the unlikely, the overlooked, and the forgotten.

And just like David, if you keep your heart set on Him, there is no limit to where He can take you.

Because in the end, it is not about where you come from, but about whom you belong to.

And you, my friend, belong to the King of Kings.

Chapter 9:
Jesus – The Greater David

The story of David is not just a historical account of an unlikely king. It is a divine foreshadowing of the coming of the ultimate King—Jesus Christ. From the fields of Bethlehem to the throne of Israel, David's life pointed forward to someone greater, someone who would establish a kingdom that would never end.

David was chosen, yet rejected. He was anointed king but spent years fleeing for his life. He was a warrior and a worshipper, a ruler and a servant. But above all, he was a man after God's own heart (1 Samuel 13:14).

Yet, as great as David was, he was only a shadow of the true King to come—Jesus Christ.

David: A Picture of the Coming King

When the people of Israel demanded a king, they wanted someone who looked the part. They wanted power, might, and strength—someone like the nations around them. So, they got Saul, a man who was physically impressive but spiritually weak.

But God had a different kind of king in mind.

David was not the choice of men. He was God's choice. And though he was rejected by many, he was the one anointed to rule.

The same pattern appears in the life of Jesus.

David was born in Bethlehem, an unlikely place for a king.

So was Jesus. (Micah 5:2, Matthew 2:1)

David was a shepherd before he became a king.

Jesus called Himself the Good Shepherd (John 10:11).

David faced rejection before his reign.
Jesus was "despised and rejected by men" (Isaiah 53:3).
David ruled Israel, but Jesus came to rule over all creation.
Everything in David's life pointed forward to the One who would establish an everlasting kingdom.

Jesus, Like David, Was Rejected Yet Chosen

Rejection is a painful experience. It wounds the soul, creates self-doubt, and often causes people to question their worth.
David understood rejection deeply.
His own father did not consider him worthy to be presented before Samuel. His brothers mocked him when he stepped up to fight Goliath. King Saul, whom he had served faithfully, turned on him and tried to kill him. Even when he finally became king, some people still doubted him.
But despite all of this, God had already chosen David.
Jesus experienced the same rejection, but on an even greater scale.
He was born into humble circumstances, not in a palace but in a manger. The religious leaders of His day refused to accept Him as the Messiah. The very people He came to save shouted, "Crucify Him!" (Matthew 27:22).
"He came to His own, and His own people did not receive Him." (John 1:11)
But just like David, Jesus was God's chosen King.
What man rejects, God exalts.
What the world despises, heaven crowns.
David sat on an earthly throne, but Jesus sits at the right hand of the Father, ruling over all things.

And the good news?
Through Jesus, we too have been chosen.

Through Christ, We Can Enter God's Presence Freely

One of the greatest moments in David's life was when he brought the Ark of the Covenant back to Jerusalem (2 Samuel 6:12-15).

The Ark represented God's presence. For years, it had been kept away, and Israel had suffered for it. But David knew that without the presence of God, nothing else mattered.

When the Ark was finally restored to its rightful place, David danced before the Lord with all his might, completely unashamed. He understood the joy of being close to God.

In the Old Testament, only priests could enter the Holy of Holies, where God's presence dwelled. But through Jesus, everything changed.

"Let us then approach God's throne of grace with confidence, so that we may receive mercy and find grace to help us in our time of need." (Hebrews 4:16)

Because of Jesus' sacrifice, we no longer need an earthly high priest to enter God's presence for us.

The curtain in the temple was torn when Jesus died (Matthew 27:51), symbolizing that access to God is now open to all who believe.

What David longed for—a closeness with God—we now have freely through Christ.

Practical Section: Understanding Our Identity in Christ

David was just a shepherd boy, overlooked and underestimated. But when God called him, he became a king.

Many people today struggle with their identity. They believe lies about who they are.
"I'm not good enough."
"I've made too many mistakes."
"I don't have what it takes."
But the story of David—and more importantly, the story of Jesus—teaches us something powerful.

- ✓ *Your identity is not based on what the world says about you.*
- ✓ *Your identity is not based on your past failures.*
- ✓ *Your identity is not based on what others think of you.*
- ✓ *Your identity is found in Christ.*

The world may see you as ordinary, but God sees you as chosen.
"You are a chosen people, a royal priesthood, a holy nation, God's special possession." (1 Peter 2:9)
Just as David went from a shepherd to a king, you have been called to something greater.

- ✓ *You are not forgotten.*
- ✓ *You are not rejected.*
- ✓ *You are not unworthy.*

Through Jesus, you are a child of God, a co-heir with Christ (Romans 8:17).
So walk in that truth.
No matter how the world sees you, God has already chosen you.
Just like He chose David.
Just like He sent Jesus.
And just like Jesus reigns as the Greater David, you are called to reign with Him.

Chapter 10:
Living a Life Glad in His Presence

There is a kind of joy that is unshakable. A joy that does not fade when life is hard. A joy that rises even in the face of trials. This joy does not come from circumstances, possessions, or achievements—it comes from being in the presence of God.

David understood this better than most. He was not a man whose life was easy or free from suffering. He was pursued by enemies, betrayed by those closest to him, and had to flee for his life on multiple occasions. Yet, through it all, David maintained one thing: his gladness in the Lord.

"In Your presence is fullness of joy; at Your right hand are pleasures forevermore." (Psalm 16:11)

David's life was a demonstration of this truth. He was a king, a warrior, a poet—but before all that, he was a worshipper. And no matter where life took him—whether in the fields as a shepherd, hiding in caves as a fugitive, or ruling from a throne—he remained glad in the presence of God.

So how can we develop that same joy? How can we live a life that is unshaken, full of thanksgiving and delight in God's presence?

David's Secret: A Life of Worship and Joy

David's joy was not dependent on his position or his possessions. It was not tied to his victories or his comfort. His joy was anchored in one thing: his relationship with God.

We see this clearly when the Ark of the Covenant was finally being brought back to Jerusalem. This was a moment of great spiritual significance. The Ark

symbolized the very presence of God among His people, and David could not contain his joy.
"Then David danced before the LORD with all his might; and David was wearing a linen ephod." (2 Samuel 6:14)
He did not care about what people thought. He was a king, yet he humbled himself before God, dancing with complete abandon because he knew the weight of what was happening. God's presence was returning to His people!
But not everyone understood David's joy. His wife, Michal, despised him for his unrestrained worship. She thought he was undignified, behaving in a way that did not befit a king. But David's response was powerful:
"I will become even more undignified than this, and I will be humiliated in my own eyes." (2 Samuel 6:22, NIV)
David knew something Michal did not. The presence of God was worth celebrating. Nothing mattered more.
What about us?
Do we have that same kind of joy in God's presence? Do we celebrate Him with all that we are, or do we hold back because we fear what others will think?
David's life challenges us to live with a heart that finds joy in God above all else.

The Power of Gratitude and Thanksgiving
The secret to lasting joy is gratitude. David was a man who understood how to give thanks, even in the hardest moments.
We see this echoed in the New Testament:

"Rejoice always, pray without ceasing, give thanks in all circumstances; for this is the will of God in Christ Jesus for you." (1 Thessalonians 5:16-18)

This verse does not say, “Give thanks for all circumstances” but rather, “Give thanks in all circumstances.” That means even when things are not going well—even when life is difficult—we can still choose gratitude.

David lived this truth.

When he was alone in the wilderness, tending sheep, he sang songs of worship.

When he was being chased by Saul, fearing for his life, he wrote psalms of trust.

When he was victorious in battle, he gave glory to God.

When he fell into sin, he repented and thanked God for His mercy.

David knew that thanksgiving shifts our focus. Instead of looking at what is missing, it reminds us of what we have. Instead of dwelling on fear, it turns our hearts to faith.

That is why the Psalms are filled with gratitude:

"Give thanks to the LORD, for He is good; His love endures forever." (Psalm 107:1)

Joy is not found in perfect circumstances. It is found in choosing gratitude daily.

Practical Steps to Walk in Joy Daily

Living in the gladness of God’s presence is not a one-time decision; it is a daily choice. Here are some practical ways to cultivate this joy in our own lives:

- ✓ Start Every Day with Thanksgiving
  Before you reach for your phone, before you check your emails, take a moment to thank God. Thank Him for life, for breath, for

salvation. Begin your day with gratitude, and it will shape your entire attitude.

- ✓ Worship Freely and Passionately
  Worship is not just about singing songs on a Sunday morning. It is a lifestyle. Worship like David—unashamed and with all your heart. Whether through music, prayer, or simply meditating on God's goodness, make worship a part of your daily life.
- ✓ Surround Yourself with Joy-Filled People
  Joy is contagious. Spend time with people who remind you of God's goodness, who encourage you in your faith, and who know how to laugh and celebrate life.
- ✓ Keep a Record of God's Faithfulness
  David wrote down his praises to God in the Psalms. You can do the same. Keep a journal of what God has done in your life. When you face challenges, look back and remember His faithfulness.
- ✓ Serve Others with a Joyful Heart
  One of the quickest ways to experience joy is to shift the focus off ourselves and onto others. Look for ways to bless and serve. Joy grows when we live with open hands.
- ✓ Pray Without Ceasing
  Stay connected to God throughout your day. Whether in the car, at work, or at home, talk to Him. Joy is found in an ongoing relationship, not just occasional encounters.

Final Challenge: Will We Respond Like David?

David's life was marked by gladness because he knew where true joy came from. He chose to worship, to give thanks, and to celebrate the presence of God.

What about us?

- ✓ *Will we dance in God's presence, even if others don't understand?*
- ✓ *Will we live a life of gratitude, no matter our circumstances?*
- ✓ *Will we choose joy daily, not based on how we feel, but based on who God is?*

The choice is ours.

David's life shows us that the presence of God is the greatest source of joy we could ever have. Nothing else compares.

So let us live like David—glad in His presence, unashamed in our worship, and full of thanksgiving all our days.

Conclusion:
A Life Marked by His Presence

As we come to the final pages of this book, take a moment to pause. Reflect. Look back on everything we have explored together—the life of David, his triumphs and failures, his unshakable trust in God, his passion for worship, his humility in repentance, and his relentless pursuit of God's presence.

David's life was not perfect, but it was marked by something greater: his deep, unbreakable relationship with God. He was a shepherd boy forgotten by his family, yet chosen by God. A mighty warrior who trembled at times, yet never stopped trusting in the Lord. A king who made grave mistakes, yet always ran back to God in repentance. His life was a testimony to God's mercy, grace, and unwavering faithfulness.

David teaches us something profound—life is not about perfection, but about pursuit. It is about chasing after God with all our hearts, no matter how many times we fall. It is about understanding that God is not looking for perfect people; He is looking for those who are willing to trust Him, love Him, and surrender to Him.

David understood this.

That is why, despite his sins and failures, God still called him "a man after My own heart" (Acts 13:22).

If there is one thing to take away from David's story, it is this: God does not measure us by our mistakes but by our response to Him. Will we run from Him, or will we run to Him? Will we let our failures define us, or will we let His grace restore us?

Rejoicing in God's Presence

One of the most defining aspects of David's life was his joy in God's presence. From the time he was a young shepherd, playing his harp under the open sky, to the day he danced before the Ark of the Covenant, David knew that being near to God was his greatest treasure.

"One thing I ask from the LORD, this only do I seek: that I may dwell in the house of the LORD all the days of my life, to gaze on the beauty of the LORD and to seek Him in His temple." (Psalm 27:4)

David did not just worship in the palace—he worshiped in the wilderness, in the caves, and in the battlefields. He did not only write songs of joy—he wrote songs of sorrow, repentance, and longing. Yet through it all, he remained close to God.

We, too, have access to this joy. We do not need to be in a church building to rejoice in God's presence. His Spirit is with us wherever we go. We can worship Him in our homes, in our workplaces, in our struggles, and in our victories. We can live every day knowing that He is near, that He is for us, and that His presence is our greatest strength.

The Mercy That Covers Us

If David's life teaches us about the joy of God's presence, it also teaches us about the depth of God's mercy.

David was not a sinless man. He committed adultery with Bathsheba and orchestrated the death of her husband. He made choices that had serious consequences. And yet, when confronted with his sin, he did not run from God—he ran to Him. He fell on his face in repentance, crying out:

"Have mercy on me, O God, according to Your unfailing love; according to Your great compassion

blot out my transgressions. Wash away all my iniquity and cleanse me from my sin." (Psalm 51:1-2)
David knew that God's mercy was greater than his failure. He knew that God's grace could restore what was broken.
And the same is true for us today.
No matter how far we have fallen, no matter what mistakes we have made, God's mercy is still greater.
This is the same mercy we see in the New Testament when Jesus tells the story of the Prodigal Son (Luke 15:11-32). A young man who squandered his inheritance in reckless living finally reached the lowest point of his life. He had nothing left. But in his brokenness, he decided to return home. And what did he find?
Not a father waiting to punish him, but a father running to embrace him.
This is the heart of God. This is the mercy that covered David. And this is the mercy that covers us today.

A Final Challenge: Will You Live Like David?
David's life was not just a story in the Bible—it is an invitation. An invitation to live a life fully surrendered to God. An invitation to:

- ✓ Worship with passion, even when others do not understand.
- ✓ Trust in God's promises, even when circumstances say otherwise.
- ✓ Run to God in repentance, knowing that His mercy is always greater.
- ✓ Delight in His presence, making Him the center of our lives.

The choice is ours.
In the book of Revelation, Jesus speaks these words:

"Behold, I stand at the door and knock. If anyone hears My voice and opens the door, I will come in and dine with him, and he with Me." (Revelation 3:20)

God is always knocking. He is always calling us deeper. He is inviting us into a life of joy, worship, and intimacy with Him.

Will we open the door?

Will we choose to live like David—running after God's heart, no matter the cost?

If you have ever felt unworthy, if you have ever doubted your place in God's plan, if you have ever wondered if God could still use you, let David's story remind you:

Yes, He can. And yes, He will.

God is looking for those who will pursue Him with all their hearts.

May you be counted among them.

May your life, like David's, be a testimony of God's faithfulness, His mercy, and His endless, unshakable love.

And may you find your greatest joy, your greatest strength, and your greatest purpose—in His presence.

About the Author 'GERARD ASSEY'

Gerard Assey is a Graduate in Economics, a PGD in Management (HRD) and holds a Doctorate in Leadership. Gerard holds several International Qualifications in Sales, Debt Collection, Training & Teaching, and is a 'Fellow' of the prestigious 'Institute of Sales & Marketing Management'-UK, a Certified NLP Practitioner, a 'Certified Trainer', an 'Accredited Management Teacher-Behavioral Sciences', a 'Certified Competency Facilitator', a 'Certified Management Consultant'- (the International credentials of a professional management consultant, awarded in accordance with global standards of the ICMCI); and a Certification from the University of Michigan in 'Successful Negotiation: Essential Strategies and Skills'

He is also a Member of the 'National Association of Sales Professionals' backed with several years experience in varied industries, both in India and Overseas. He also holds an 'Etiquette Consultant' Certification from the USA (by Sue Fox, Author of Best Seller: 'Business Etiquette for Dummies'. She has trained some of the top celebrities' world over). He was also a recipient of a scholarship for extensive training in Japan on 'Corporate Management for India'.

Gerard Assey is 'Founder & Chief Corporate Trainer' of the Group: **'Citius, Altius, Fortius Unlimited'**- an organization that **celebrated 20 years of Glorious Service** in 2021, focusing on 3 Core Competencies:

People. Performance. Profit; in functional areas of Sales & Marketing, HR & Organizational Development, covering Recruitment, Training & Consultancy!

Having managed organizations with large Sales Forces in India & Overseas, his specialization cover extensive areas of Sales Training (All levels - Presentation, Negotiation, Key/ Strategic Accounts Management & Managerial Skills for all sectors), Bid Proposal/ Capture Planning/ Management Trainings, Retail Sales, Customer Service & Customer Retention Programs, Training for Prevention & Collection of Debt, Self & Personal Development Programs (Time Management, Teamwork & Team Building, Business Etiquette & Personal Grooming, Leadership & Managerial Skills, People Management Skills, Train-the-Trainer etc), including preparation of Custom-designed Business Manuals for Internal (HR, Induction, and Sales etc) & External use (Instruction, User Manuals).

Gerard has successfully conducted over 6450 Trainings & Workshops (as of April '25) all across India, Middle East, Africa, Europe & S.E. Asia. Besides public programs conducted regularly, both in India & Overseas, he has some of the top names as clients whom he services from Single Owners to large Public & Government undertakings, covering all sectors, for their in-house needs.

His website: www.CollectionSkills.com is the only one in this part of the world to be featured in the 'Collections & Credit Risk Magazine-USA' under 'Who's Who in Training' and ranks TOP, along with other websites listed below on most search engines.

Gerard is author of 185 books already (April 2025), all the books being available on all online platforms and outlets as E-books and Paperbacks

A few of our business related books:

1. Bite-sized Bits on Commonsense Management
2. Heart to Heart on Life's Principles'
3. How to become a Successful Manager
4. The Sales Professionals' Master Workbook of S.Y.S.T.E.M.S
5. The Professional Business Email Etiquette Handbook & Guide
6. The Professional Business Video-Conferencing Etiquette Handbook & Guide
7. Professional Presentation Skills
8. Exceptional Customer Service
9. Professional Tele-Marketing Skills
10. Professional Debt Collection Skills
11. The G.R.E.A.T. Sales & Service Workbook
12. Sales Training Advantage for Results (*The Ultimate Sales Training Manual to enable you stand out as a S.T.A.R.*)
13. CEO Daily Planner & Organizer
14. The Sales Professionals' Master Daily Planner
15. The Professional Debt Collector's Master Daily Planner
16. My Daily Planner & Organizer
17. MY EMERGENCY INFORMATION RECORD (Family Emergency & Peace of Mind Planner)
18. The Ultimate Therapist & Counselors Planner and Organizer
19. Building an Ethical Workplace
20. Managing Relationships at Work
21. Managing Business Meetings Effectively
22. Effective Delegation Skills
23. Goal Setting for Success
24. B2B Selling by Email
25. Professional Business Etiquette & Grooming
26. Dining Etiquette & Table Manners
27. Effective Networking Skills
28. Grooming, Etiquette & Manners for Teens, Young Adults & Future Leaders
29. Inter-Personal Skills
30. Get Ready, Get Hired!
31. Selling in a Recession

32. Effective Receivables Management in an Economic Downturn!
33. Real Estate & Property Sales Training
34. Credit Sales & Accounts Receivable Management
35. Selling Skills for Real Estate & Property Advisors
36. Take G.R.E.A.T. C.A.R.E!
37. Spa, Salon & Health Club Selling Skills
38. Selling Travel, Holiday & MICE Services
39. Selling Skills for Spa's, Salons & Health Clubs
40. Retailing in Salons & Spas
41. Selling Holiday, Vacation, Tours & Packages
42. The Power of Sales Referrals
43. Selling Luxury
44. Technical Selling Skills
45. Financial Advisors Sales Training
46. Dealing with Burnout at Work Monopolize Your Markets
47. Selling to Affluent Customers
48. Growing up with Grace
49. Financial Selling Skills
50. *The Effective Manager's Guide: Key Skills to Thrive*
51. From Aspiring to Inspiring: A Guide for New Managers on the Rise
52. The Power of Focus
53. Selling with Integrity: Sell Like Jesus The Perfect Role Model!
54. 31 Habits of Champions: Your 31-Day Journey to Greatness
55. Rejecting Grasshopper Talk: From Grasshopper to Giant-Killer-*Defeating Giants Daily!*
56. Navigate the AI-Powered Future of Bid & Proposals: Up-Skill to Stay Relevant with Alternative Career Paths & Opportunities
57. Hiring Sales Winners
58. Present with Impact
59. Success Unlocked: *Breaking Free from Habits that Hold You Back*
60. Complaints to Cheers, Feedback to Gold: Mastering Complaints Management
61. Thriving Together: *Cultivating Diversity, Equity, and Inclusion*
62. Coaching Skills for Sales Managers

63. Soaring to Success in Business & Leadership: Swifter, Higher, Stronger!
64. From Classroom to Podium: A Student's Guide to Powerful Public Speaking & Presentation Skills
65. Developing Self-Discipline
66. The CEO's 31-Day Power Plan: Unlocking Success through Essential Traits
67. Credibility Matters
68. A Winning Attitude
69. Bid & Proposal Management Using AI
70. Sales Forecasting: A Practical & Proven Guide to Strategic Sales Forecasting
71. Elevate & Energize: *50 Dynamic & Fun Activities for Peak Workplace Morale*
72. 'Sales SOS! Sales on Fire! *30 Days to Conquer Chaos & the Nightmares of Success!'*
73. Mastering Sales Managerial Skills: *Building High-Performing Teams & Driving Exceptional Results*
74. Eagle-Eyed Leadership: Unleashing the Power of 31 Lessons from Eagles
75. The Ultimate Employee Training Guide: *Training Today, Leading Tomorrow*
76. Being More Accountable at Work
77. Creating a Culture of Continuous Improvement
78. Effective Questioning & Listening Skills
79. The Power of Value Selling
80. The Growth Mindset
81. Mastering Professional Help Desk Skills
82. The Power to Lead with Empathy
83. Being Prepared: The Key to Unlocking Success
84. Youthful Spark-Youth Energizers, Activities and Games-Igniting the Fun in Youth
85. Ignite your Motivation for Success
86. Elevate Your Executive Presence: *Your Roadmap to Executive Excellence*
87. Smart Decisions: *Mastering Problem Solving with Strategic Solutions for Business Success*
88. Strategic Planning: *Developing and Implementing Strategic Plans to Achieve Long-Term Business Goals*
89. The Power of Stay Interviews
90. Developing G.R.I.T.
91. Adaptability

92. Diagnosis- *A Key Skill for Leadership*
93. The Burnout-Proof Salesperson: *The Master Guide to Preventing Stress & Burnout-* Strategies for Thriving in Sales
94. Learning from Failure: *Keys to Success*
95. Customer Success Management
96. Overcoming the Killers of Motivation
97. The C-Suite Code: *Mastering Skills for Executive Excellence'*
98. Dealing with Difficult Customers
99. Unlocking Your Potential: Mastering the Top 20 Life Skills for a Brighter Future
100. Nurturing Tomorrow's Leaders: *Essential Soft Skills Every Child Must Learn*
101. Lively & Fun Party Games for Seniors & Elders
102. Role Playing for Sales Champions: From Practice to Performance
103. Fun and Exciting Party Games for Kids
104. Case Studies for Sales
105. Role-Playing for Unbeatable Customer Service
106. Case Studies in Customer Service
107. Case Studies in Winning Negotiations
108. Case Studies in Management & Leadership
109. Case Studies in Human Resources & Talent Management
110. CEO Success Blueprint: The Essential Toolkit for CEOs and C-Level Executives
111. The Salesperson's Self-Coaching Guide: *Master Your Own Self-Coaching Plan for Success*
112. Overcoming Procrastination: *Your Ultimate Guide to Stop Delaying and Start Living Your Best Life*
113. When True Colors Are Exposed: *The Journey to Unmasking Humanity*
114. Life-Changing Habits for Teens: Teen Success Blueprint for a Bright Future
115. Workplace Stress-Free: *Proven Strategies to Thrive at Work and Beyond*
116. Objection Overruled: *The Ultimate Guide to Turning 'No' into 'Yes'*

From the Ministry side, Gerard graduated in the very first batch of Charis Bible College-India & had for over 9 years served as a Part-time Faculty at Charis Bible College-Chennai (Andrew Wommack Ministries-Colorado, USA).
He is also a graduate of the Advanced Mentorship Program (AMP) and the Circle Of Ministerial Engagement (C.O.M.E.) of Prophet Jerome Fernando and a Spiritual Son of the Esteemed Prophet.
An accomplished author of several Secular & Christian Books, Gerard has been on the board of a few international organizations and boasts of being the SON of the MOST HIGH GOD: An ordinary guy following an extraordinary GOD!

...And some of his most recent Christian Books being:

1. A Bouquet of Praises for My KING
2. Christian Jokes for the Serious Religious' Folks!
3. Jesus Healed You!
4. Praise24Ever! (also in Tamil version)
5. The 5G Network of GOD
6. Building Faith over F.E.A.R- FACE EVERYTHING AND RISE with JESUS
7. Hebrew and Greek Praise and Worship Words
8. Godly Mothers' and Grandmothers' Bible Story time for Kids!
9. Miracles of Jesus in Pictures
10. Raise your Praise all 365 Days
11. Thanking GOD with an Attitude of Gratitude
12. Meditating on the Attributes of GOD
13. Puppet Scripts
14. Alcohol Ruins, JESUS Reforms, Renews & Restores!
15. Habakkuk 2:2 Christian Daily Journal, Planner & Organizer
16. ABC of GOD's Word for Handwriting Practice
17. Daily Bible Verse Handwriting Practice (Building Godly Character & Faith through Cursive Handwriting Practice!)
18. Guiding Light: Fun & Faith-Building Bible Activities for Children
19. Rejecting Grasshopper Talk: From Grasshopper to Giant-Killer-*Defeating Giants Daily!*
20. Teen Titans of Faith: *Building Courage, Determination & Christ-like-Esteem*
21. I AM Empowered: *Unleashing Divine Power with Positive Declarations*
22. Be A Solution Provider-*From Passion to Purpose*: *A Biblical Guide to Being the Answer to the World!*
23. Miracles of JESUS

24. Parables of Jesus for a Meaningful Life!
25. A Grateful Heart: Importance of Sharing Testimonies of GOD's Grace
26. Melodies of Worship to JESUS: 31 Songs of Praise & Worship From My Heart to HIS!
27. I AM SO BLESSED!
28. My Daily Cup of Energizer
29. 31 Leadership Lessons *from* Jesus- *The Supreme Leader*
30. Peace Amidst Storms: A Biblical Guide to Conquering S.T.R.E.S.S.
31. Rise Above: 20 Biblical Eagle Lessons for Life's Triumphs
32. Godly Goal Setting: *The FAITHFUL Blueprint for a Purpose-Driven Life*
33. The Profound Attributes of our Mighty GOD: Understanding the 10S's of the Almighty
34. Worship Now, Worship Forever: *A Journey from Earthly Praise to Eternal Glory*
35. Unceasing Praise & Worship: *365 Days to Worship the King*
36. The ROAR Within: *Living with Purpose and Authority through the Power of the Holy Spirit*
37. From Potential to Purpose: Unlocking and Multiplying Your Talents & Gifts for Kingdom Impact
38. Songs from the Heart: *Worshipping GOD in Your Own Tune & Melody*
39. Awakening Praise & Worship: Hebrew & Greek Words to Raise Your Praise
40. Sing a NEW Song to the LORD Everyday: *Daily Devotions of Praise & Worship to Lift Your Heart & Glorify HIS Name*
41. *The* A.R.O.M.A. of True Worship: *Creating Worship That Delights God*
42. Becoming A Kingdom Champion: *Embracing God's Call for a Life of Purpose & Victory*
43. The Busy Businessman's Daily Devotional: 366 Crisp Truths to Start Your Day Strong
44. The Teacher's Heart: *Daily Devotions for Educators*
45. Anchored! *A 31-Day Devotional for Students Facing Life's Challenges*
46. Suddenly! Unlocking Unorthodox Breakthroughs through Unusual Worship
47. Overcoming Adversity: *Lessons from the Bible for Modern Challenges*
48. LORD, Don't do it without me
49. Kingdom Leadership: *Biblical Principles for Modern Leaders*
50. Heartprints of God- *Growing God's Way:* Daily Devotions for Kids

to Shine Bright

51. Send Judah First: Let your Praises Go up First to See the Mighty Move of GOD
52. DIVINE MOMENTS: *Recognizing, Embracing, Preparing, and Walking into Life-Changing Encounters with God*
53. Be a Builder in the Kingdom: *The C.E.M.E.N.T. Guide to Creating a Lasting Legacy*
54. Unshakable: *Pillars of Godly Womanhood* (Pillars of Faith That Changed History)
55. Lead Like a Shepherd: *14 Essential Traits for Pastoral Excellence*
56. The Worship Leader's Arsenal: *Powerful Exhortations to Ignite Thanksgiving, Praise & Worship*
57. Women of UnShakable Faith: *31-Day Devotional for Strength, Purpose & Influence*
58. Called to Teach: *A Complete 10-Week Training Guide for Impactful VBS Teachers*
59. Strumming for the KING: Cowboy Songs of Faith & Fire
60. The Ultimate Youth Camp Playbook: *50 Bible-Centered Indoor Games to Engage, Equip, and Empower Teens*
61. Glad in HIS Presence: *David's Revelation of GOD's Love & Mercy*

Besides regularly contributing to business & trade journals, including international ones such as the 'Creative Training Techniques' and the 'Sales News' of the U.S.A, He is also a member of several prestigious bodies & trade associations, having participated in many Conferences & Workshops in India & Overseas.

Prior to his last assignment of leading & managing a large MNC as head, Gerard had a 3-year stint in the Middle East as a Consultant with a leading British Consultancy Firm.

As the past 'Official Country Representative' for the International Business Award- 'THE STEVIES'-(the business world's own Oscar) for about 4 years- he ensured a few Indian companies that qualify for the same every year!

Gerard can be contacted at:

Email: training@Sales-Training.in,training@CollectionSkills.com
Websites:

www.Sales-Training.in
www.EtiquetteWorks.in
www.CollectionSkills.com
www.RetailSalesTraining.in
www.SalesTrainingIndia.com
www.ManualPreparation.com
www.TrainingWithPuppets.com
www.FirstContactAcademy.com
www.SalesAndMarketingRecruiter.com

Our TRAININGS that can help your team

- ✓ **Sales Effectiveness**: Selling Skills for any Sector: Service/ Logistics/ FMCG Realty/ Insurance & Finance/ Media/ SPA's, Health Clubs & Salons/ Key Account Management, Effective Negotiation Skills/ Bid & Proposal Management Skills/ Retail Sales Training: Any Sector (Auto, Jewelry, Clothing, Luxury etc)
- ✓ **Customer Service Skills**-Complaints Handling & Customer Retention
- ✓ **Debt Prevention & Collection Skills**
- ✓ **Etiquette & Grooming**
- ✓ **Leadership & Managerial Skills**
- ✓ **Self & Personal Development Skills**: Presentation Skills/ Effective Communication Skills/Business Proposal Writing Skills/ Problem Solving & Decision Making Skills/ Empowering Secretaries-The perfect PA! (For Secretaries & PA's)/ Effective Time Management/ Teamwork & Teambuilding/ P.R.I.D.E- **P**ersonal **R**esponsibility **I**n **D**elivering **E**xcellence

www.ingramcontent.com/pod-product-compliance
Ingram Content Group UK Ltd.
Pitfield, Milton Keynes, MK11 3LW, UK
UKHW021341190726
13845UKWH00027B/672

9 788198 569165